Black Wings

# BLACK WINGS

## Len Roberts

The National Poetry Series 1989
Selected by Sharon Olds

Persea Books
New York

I thank the editors of the following magazines in which some of these poems first appeared: *Carolina Quarterly, Cincinnati Review, Exquisite Corpse, Indiana Review, Michigan Quarterly Review, The North American Review, Northwest Review, Passages North, Pennsylvania Review, Poetry, Prairie Schooner, Seattle Review, Southern Poetry Review, Tar River Poetry Review, Three Rivers Poetry Review, West Branch.*

I also thank the National Endowment for the Arts and the Pennsylvania Council on the Arts for grants of financial assistance during the years these poems were written. My thanks also to Yaddo for residencies which gave me the time and peace to write. I am especially indebted to Hayden Carruth and Gerald Stern for their continual support and advice, and to Tony Hoagland for his helpful insights into the arrangement of the poems in this manuscript. And many thanks to Nancy for her patience and help.                                                L.R.

For information, address the publisher:

Persea Books, Inc.
60 Madison Avenue
New York, New York 10010

Library of Congress Cataloging-in-Publication Data

Roberts, Len, 1947–
    Black wings : poems / Len Roberts.
        p. cm. —(The National poetry series)
    ISBN 0-89255-141-0 : $9.95
    I. Title. II. Series.
PS3568.02389B5      1989                                              89-2972
811'.54—dc19                                                              CIP

Set in Bembo by Keystrokes, Lenox, Massachusetts
Manufactured in the United States of America

First Edition

# CONTENTS

I

# THE RED LEAVES REMIND ME AGAIN

we've set the clocks back, gained
another hour, a cold one, looks like,
the thermometer reading 34 degrees
and droppng. My three-year-old
jumps into the pile I've raked
under the maple, yells that we
should go get some yellow ones, he
knows where they are, in the town
park, big, perfect yellow ones
we could mix in with these boring
reds. Then he's off into the beginning
dark, toward the shimmering forsythia
leaves that have not fallen yet, and
when he turns I can hardly see
his face afloat in the dim gray, think
I will soon need glasses to see distances, too,
like my father who has been dead
these eighteen years. And I remember the parking lot of
    the hospital,
sitting on the yellow curb, watching leaves whirl
against the fence, old, brown oak
leaves that rattled until I woke
from the daze I was in, realized
my father would be dead soon, and so
went up to see him in the cold November light.

## WITHOUT TAKING OFF HIS COAT

my father calls me over, asks
me to sit on his lap while he shows
the ivory cufflinks and tie pin,
the gold R glittering in their
centers. Then he starts to rock
on the linoleum, making it creak
in time to his whistling as we
watch the winter light outside
the blind-windows turn silver
then dark. He is my father
and holds me to his chest, rubs
the soft skin of my face, my neck
as he whispers snatches of song I can
never remember until I'm alone
in bed. Once upon a time, he
begins, and The fox knew better
than to forget, and then, always,
The end, The end, while outside
tires swish in the snow and the
streetlight blinks on, brings
shadows into the kitchen where
we sit and rock in what light
is left.

# TEN BELOW

Ten below and I followed my mother
in her patch-quilt bathrobe down Remsen
and Ontario, under the Black Bridge
encased in ice, past Freighofer's
stables where the horses' breath rose
to steam the dim yellow windows. Miles
she strode, calling out the name of her brother
who had played amateur baseball before
Korea, her sister with one leg gone, snow
falling on her shoulders, turning her rollered
hair white. Stretching my legs
to step in her prints, I held back
at corners when she stopped to curse
the red doors of the closed church,
the neon bull glowing from Boney's Bar.
An old couple walked by, their eyes down,
a car with chains rattled on the cobblestones,
but my mother was already gone
across the railroad tracks, to the island
and Little League field where she squatted
and yanked the pad out, let her blood
drip into the snow, small dark holes I
could see from the dugout less than thirty
feet away. Then she yelled the names
again and I knew I would have to run
soon for my father, pound on the door until
he woke, hold the blankets and thermos
while we waited for the car to warm up.
But for now I was a statue, hardening
in the wind and snow, tightening,
drawing into myself until I could not feel
my feet, my hands or face, and my breath
barely steamed the iron-cold air
where my mother lay.

# REMOVING THE MOLE

As I felt the doctor cut the mole
out of my left leg, birthmark in the same
place my mother had hers, I remembered
the dark kitchen on White Street, the picture
of her standing by the cupboard, a slice
of white bread covered with sugar in one hand,
a butter knife in the other. I saw again
the rollers in her hair, the quilted bathrobe
she wore over flannel pajamas, her sunken
eyes and full lips, the pug nose, the poverty
of her, the loss of her mind there in that kitchen,
and I wondered if the man taking the picture
had felt it, the one who had to focus in the dark,
who had to wait in the dark until she had spread the bread
with butter and sprinkled the sugar, the one who said
nothing until he snapped the bulb, throwing
light all over her otherwise disguised face,
catching her like an animal in its dark hole,
her half-crooked Oh telling him what he did not want
        to know.

# WHITE FLOWER

She stands in the middle, four
soldiers with their arms around her
neck, her waist, her shoulders. One leg
is raised on the wooden step slightly higher
than the other, a jauntiness at seventeen. The picture
has browned but her eyes gleam brighter
than the brass on her collar, and she is smiling,
this woman who has no idea she will be my mother.
For now she is Georgia, away from the cobblestones
and hard bread of the rowhouse. For now
she is beautiful with hair curled and lipstick
on. I imagine that night she walks
into the moon of some warm field and lies down
with one of the men—she is so happy
in her white skin that she sings.
Near her face a white flower, a delicate stem
and small head, petals shaped like tears,
the thin tips near the dark center. I want her
to smell the white flower, to reach out those few
inches with her right hand and touch it, gently,
before rising to enter her life.

# LEARNING ON OLMSTEAD STREET

The tattoo of a heart with an arrow
piercing it has MOTHER written in blue
across the pink center, and it moves
each time my father piles another stack
of coins on the kitchen table or reaches
to lift the gold glass of beer. Who was the
sixth president, he asks, the capital of Idaho,
Nebraska, What's the difference between
the Arctic and Anarctic, the change
for two boxes of doughnuts at twenty-three
cents each if the man hands me a five-
dollar bill? Even as I stand to wrap
sandwiches in waxed paper, folding
the corners in neat triangles the way
he taught me, he asks the names
of the last three governors of New York,
says in French I've dropped the knife.
Bending to pick it up, he's suddenly
beside me, his eyes bloodshot,
his breath blue smoke as he repeats
the average life span of an ant, a moth,
then wipes up the stain in looping
figure eights, the sign for infinity
he says, tossing me the dirty cloth.

# RISING TO WORK

My father made his small noises
in the kitchen again, the quick shuffle
of stockinged feet across linoleum, hiss
of water into the pot, then the low
tunes of the radio sifting into my room
with the dim yellow that flickered from
      the kitchen wall.
I could tell by the light behind the blinds
that snow was falling, thick, wet flakes,
which made my father sit more still
than usual at the white table
before he shaved, the click of his breadman's purse
muffled in his shirt. He was judging the curves
in the road, how many inches of ice beneath,
he was lifting the heavy white cup of coffee
carefully to his mouth, carefully setting it down.
For seconds we stayed like that, my head lifted
from the pillow so I could hear, his quiet body
sitting on the kitchen chair, legs crossed,
smoke drifting from his nose, both of us
waiting in that peace before we stirred,
sheathed by large, white flakes that whirled
in the slapping cold where my father's Golden
      Eagle bread truck idled.

# IN THE KITCHEN

After he came home sobbing from the pool,
she took his shirt and shorts off, the blue
sneakers and socks, then lifted
him onto the table, under the one bulb.
Bending to peer at his thighs, where the bite
marks were, the teeth curved in red and a beginning
bruise, she spread his cheeks apart, held his
penis and rolled his balls in the palm
of her hand, all the while whispering Now
he'll be queer. When her voice stopped
we could hear him, white and stiff in that August
night, the breaths rasping as though his lungs
had grown into an old man's in those few hours,
in and out, the ribs of his chest like the hull
of some ship heaving its way through a storm.

# SHE GOES OUT TO BUY GROCERIES

Mother out in the snow
to buy onions and potatoes, her brown boots
making small tracks off the porch, her back
like a target as it nears Ontario Avenue.
I see her in the Food Circus's afterglow,
white hands testing the hothouse tomatoes, rolling
the lettuce as she eyes the pig's feet, the caviar.
No one there knows she's waited two years
with both hands on the sill, no one knows
the nights she stuffed the pillow
between her legs to stop the flow.
No one sees the soft, round face, the tongue
tired of white buttered bread sprinkled
with sugar, wanting the thick cream
of eclairs, the red meat of steak. So well
she contains the butcher knife, the dreams
of the river, as she pushes the silver
cart from aisle to aisle, marking
on the small white pad the cost
of every bag and can she picks up.

## WE

I see her lying in the dark
of St. John's Alley, her mother and father
downstairs at the table, eating cake they would not
    share with their nine children,
the young boy next to her smoking, his head propped
up on one arm, talking to her and her refusing
    to answer.
She was fourteen and had breasts
that I can feel hang from me now as they must
have hung from her when she turned onto her stomach,
their weight throwing her off-balance just enough
    to notice.
And my hand is the boy's hand, reaching out in the dark
to touch them, hard, full, playing with the nipples
until she became excited, felt the soft giving
    begin
that she would not stop for the rest of her life.
There we are, lovers, the boy and I watching
her leave the child she was behind, watching her
move into the rhythm of her years, twisting,
jerky movements that rocked the bed, her eyes
closed as I, he, we rise on top of her
and break her apart.
              What is love
if not this, she taught me all those years
in the hallway as she swung the broom again,
broke it over my back, kicked me when I went down,
ten, forcing me, after, to put my arm around her shoulder,
her white body trembling in the silvery mirror,
my body standing beside her, perfectly still.

# R. R. R.

*"Yet why not say what happened?"*
—Robert Lowell, from "Epilogue"

My father's name was Raymond,
Raymond Richard Roberts, R. R. R.,
I used to whisper him at night
when I lay awake, thinking
that he could have been
a railroad, or a building,
the R & R & R pulling into
the Cohoes Freight Yard,
the R & R & R Paperbag Factory,
his initials carrying me down
rails that shone with possibility,
sweet blueberry bushes to one side,
young Irene, in the green bathing suit,
    waiting for me at the quarry.
Downstairs he slept with an angry
    woman who would not let
him touch her, who stared at the tin
    ceiling
those mornings he would say
    the presidents
and I would give their dates,
when he shouted out the capitals
    and I shouted back the states,
when he called me Leonard, the Lion-
    Heart,
and I called him Raymond, Raymond, Raymond,
    ignorant
until years later, long after
his death, that his name
stemmed from Raginmund,
Frankish, for *to counsel, to protect.*

# THE SEVEN STEPS

Uncles gather about the coffee pot,
aunts peer into their purses for whatever
they've lost while mother sits in the large
green chair, shaking the many hands that
float in front of her face. In the other room
my father lies stiff in his last gray
suit, the swirled paisley tie nearly making
me sick when I sneak in again to stare at the
halfmoons of his fingernails. Yellow
and red and white flowers bloom all around him
while Uncle Jack talks about the machine gun
at Guam, at Guadalcanal, the Panama Zone, the old
story of the dead man lost on an island for two years
with snakes tied around his long hair, jungle
rot holes eating his skin. Aunt Bea
remembers how he could smell the weather,
whispers just a few days ago a pigeon
looked in her window at him and she knew
he was in trouble. But only I
have the black eyes and long fingers, the left
eyebrow that curves up toward the high
ceiling, only I know the seven steps to take
when he plays the harmonica, which I practice
as I weave among them, a secret
he showed me, perfecting myself.

II

# VIC

★★★

Vic heard a plane and looked up, thought
a bomb was about to drop, but
he saw nothing except goldenrod
and chickory and Queen Anne's Lace quietly
exploding, quick bursts in the sun that
cast shadows, and in those shadows other
bursts of stone and dirt so brilliant he
had to close his eyes and wait. When he opened
them, he saw his son by the barn, his entire
back blistering, his head on fire,
that yellow-white globe glowing around it.
Tasting the iron in his mouth, Vic prayed
this was just another one of his fits
as he kept cutting the grass, but
his wife writhed down there behind
the house where she hung bright
clothes on the line, flinging
her hands and arms all about
as though she were engulfed
by a cloud of hornets. Then the blast waves
rippled like simple heat across the field;
and the stone row, the black walnuts and poison
sumacs lifted a few inches from
the trembling earth, nearly jolting
Vic off the gleaming red Jacobsen,
even though the sky was blue, without
one cloud, and the white blustering blooms
of the apple tree were full and perfectly still.

\*\*\*

Sucking oxygen in the bedroom,
Vic listened to Elvis sing his five
albums again, thinking of Bunny,
his sexy girlfriend, and Jeannine, the reliable
one with a car, his big wave combed
up those nights he roller-skated home
from Guptill's Arena without braking once.
Love me tender, Elvis sang, and Vic
put out his hands to feel the heavy
breasts, imagined unbuttoning the green
brocaded dress the night of the school
dance. Then Mary on the brown carpet
that morning before work when both
her parents had gone, the guys in the car
blowing the horn. Rows of pills
on the shelf, his collection of copper
shone in the little sun, and Vic got
up to piss, saw his wavering face staring
back from the toilet water, missing
teeth, the oldness still surprising
as he bent to flush it all down the drain,
wanting to hum as he stepped carefully back
to the bed, but staying quiet,
afraid to give himself away.

\*\*\*

Vic walked past the barn, the five
cord of hardwood split and stacked
for winter, up to where he was lost
again in the ice that gleamed on the tops
of branches, shimmered on wheat stalks
and old goldenrod, everywhere he looked

the shining that made him bend
and pull a stalk up, bite gently
down to crack the ice sheath, tongue
it into his mouth. Just
yesterday he was gone
into one of his fits, unable to say a word,
able only to sit at the white table
and smoke packs of cigarettes, drink
coffee from the heavy white cup. All
day he'd watched the snow pile up
and last night, when he let the cats out
into the five below zero, he saw
his dead father again, lurching
drunkenly through the snow, Vic's mother
following in the blue bathrobe,
and behind her the two boys, silent.
He watched until they passed
the pond and went out of sight, saw
they left no tracks, and so said nothing
when he came back into the house,
just lay in bed feeling the dark
upon him, deciding he would look
for them again tomorrow morning,
soon as daylight broke.

★★★

The night kept getting colder
as Vic set the alarm for twelve,
three and six in order to tend the fire,
unable to sleep in between, watching
his infant son breathe, bumping
his knee twice into the coffee table
because he did not want to turn on the light.
At the window he saw countless ice

bursts gleaming, bunched tightly together
as though in wreaths at a funeral parlor,
and he thought of his long-dead father, getting
up only to drink whiskey the former tenant
had forgotten to take. He no longer
knew the woman sleeping in bed, the place
he called home just brought figures
of money into his head, and when he asked himself
what he loved, he could answer the boy, the snow,
sometimes music, sometimes for a few
weeks or months a woman in a strange apartment
where he came to know a past pieced
together by random words and long stretches
of silence. What he didn't know or love was
out there, the storm that whirled
and twisted in iron-cold black air
that he stared at until the empty face
in the glass began staring back, and he gave
up again, turned to throw another log
into the snapping mouth of the stove.

★★★

Vic hands me my coat and gloves, says
he wants to show me the barn, the six acres
he ploughs, the five cord of wood, all
hand-split, his hands, his ax. Out
in below zero, he looks for his wife in the window,
walks with another man's steps, toes
pointing in, like a pigeon's, like our
father's, whose ghost skulks around the house
at night, Vic whispers, especially
in winter, just one light on in the kitchen
where Vic likes to sit and smoke. In
the darker shadows of the barn, he flashes

the light on the bodies of rabbits
hung from the beam, their empty
skins swinging easily in the wind
that knocks slate dust down from the roof.
Blood, he says, pulling out his knife
to hack a leg off, one or two drops forming
on the thigh, the fur stiff, hard as a brush
Vic makes me touch and then says
Dad puts his face upon his face
at night and breathes fearful dreams
into his head. By flashlight beam
I see Vic's eyes are our father's eyes,
his nose, his teeth, even the voice now
becoming that low rumble as he moves deeper
into the barn where he keeps
the cows and one horse, turning around
just once, the light held by his face,
afloat in the dark.

# TALKING TO THE POISON SUMAC

Bending the poison sumac down to my lips
I told it the name of my older brother,
the one with the mad light of winter
in his eyes, who could not walk up a flight
of steps without stopping to catch
his breath, and I looked into the hard buds,
pried a few up, long narrow pits of poison
I let drop, let the branch
spring back into the cold sky. Soon he
would whirl away like that, leave his
thirty years on the V. A.'s iron bunk,
hundreds of electric shocks, the innumerable
pills, that, at the beginning, he
liked the colors of, would call me
in another state to say he was now taking
the green-yellow-blue, the white-red-black,
laughing at the sickness he had become.
And I didn't know why I was out there
thinking of his soft body I had not held
for more than twenty years, repeating
his story when I knew that nothing
I did or said mattered, that the sky
was powerless, and the sun setting
powerless, that the snow that started
to fall, the beautiful falling
itself, was nothing, the field, the world,
the unlivable, burning stars, the emptiness
of it all contained here in one small human heart.

III

# WHEN THE BISHOP CAME

These angels were messengers
of the Lord, we were told as we sat
in straight pews they had brought
into the classroom because
the Bishop was coming with his ring
and miter, so he could see
who could answer the sacred questions
from the heavenly blue
Baltimore Catechism,
Jimmy Legasse and Joseph McGraw
in front because they were smart,
followed by Gabriella Wells and Irene
Tousignant, their dresses pressed
and hair curled in rolls Donald Wilcox
always put his fingers into, Donald
who stayed after school every day
because he was sloppy, fat, and cursed,
Donald, whose eyes were a quiet gray
even that day Father slammed him
from wall to wall of the yellow
cafeteria, none of us knew
for what. And it was Donald
the Bishop saw, the black sheep
so obvious in that fourth-grade
flock, and it was Donald he asked
the Nine Beatitudes, the Cardinal
Sins, the Apostles, even, finally,
the Pope's name, Donald
who did not get one answer right,
whose flesh turned that translucent
pig-pink with shame or fear or grace

when the Bishop walked down to his last
pew in the last row by the window
and put his gem-studded-sparkling
ring out, which Donald held up to the sun
to see sacred streaks of light flash
before he bowed his head and kissed.

# PUSHING CARS OUT OF THE SNOW

Pushing the yellow Cougar out of the snow,
its tires spinning muddy slush onto
my good pants, I remember all the men
back on Olmstead Street coming out
at dawn when someone's car was stuck,
or later, in the evening, when a stranger
slid into the gully near the canal, how
their jackets would steam from
the kitchen heat as they strode out
to push and shove and joke. Tremblay,
Dumas, Heroux, Polisviet, Campbell,
all of the men with pipes are gone
into the snow that keeps falling,
their boot tracks filling as soon
as they leave them, their backs
snow-filmed, overloading the air
as they walked down the street after
pushing the car from the rut, some of them
clapping snow from their red
hands, some of them looking up
at the sky that had turned to snow,
shaking their heads as though
saying No, No, with the greatest pleasure.

# LEARNING TO DANCE

My younger brother whirled and tapped
on the cracked linoleum, swooped to a bow
and then sat on an invisible seat
to cross his hands from knee to knee,
his favorite trick. Then my older brother,
gold watch and gold ring gleaming, clicked
clicked around the white table to where I sat.
My father kept playing but I couldn't dance,
my legs winding into each other, heel coming down
    instead of toe,
arms waving in circles just to keep me up.
My father said nothing but did not stop
when I stumbled and fell, he wouldn't
slow down when I whirled into the wall,
and in his musical silence I yelled
I can't, I can't, and I felt
his disbelief rise up in that kitchen
until it was thick as the snow
that fell outside in the twenty below.
It was that light, rhythmical falling
finding its way through the blinds
that saved me that morning, that lifted
me up from my awkward knees to the height
of my dancing, that whirled me with the gift
    I had been given at birth
but had forgotten in the early hours
    of the milk route,
the long days of colored flash cards
raised in the fifth-grade classroom,
and I tapped for a good minute,

and my brothers watched, as dumbfounded
    as I,
while my father kept playing, his thin lips
    tight,
blowing the life they had left
    into the awkward one.

# THE SINNER IN ST. BERNARD'S

(for Linda Bouchard)

That dark afternoon in St. Bernard's
when the foreign priest screamed as I
    confessed,
I had to walk out into the suffering
    light of saints
sifting from the stained glass windows
    down
to every face I knew in Cohoes staring
    back
at the recognized sinner. Father,
    forgive me, I had begun,
I've touched a girl's breast by the river,
and stolen and lied, I've taken the name
    of the Lord and my mother
in vain, and I've watched the naked girls
sit fully dressed in geometry class
poring over right angles and perfect circles,
Maureen without her matching skirt and blouse,
Sylvia sitting up straight by the crumpled
    pastel-blue dress, and
I had them there, on the red-painted floor
    of my imagination
where I burn daily, Lord, but especially
at night in Danny's Pizzeria, when
their loveliness hangs down in the form
of Mary Magdalene, or Delilah, or Donna
who attacked me in the silver-gray Chevy,
who ripped the buttons off my shirt. Staggering
    out of the confessional's curtain, blinded
by the new light, I heard the priest furiously
    pounding

on the dark screen, screaming behind me
No Absolve, No Absolve, Repent, Repent,
        maybe next week, . . .
trying to scare me with the Fires of Hell
that blazed before me from the mural on the
        church wall
which I glided by as quickly as I could,
not wanting the good people who waited
        in line for forgiveness
to know who I was, at fifteen, a young
man marked with the black ashes of the cross
        on his unwrinkled forehead,
the black ashes of lust already mounding
        in his heart
that yearned, My God, for the silvery light
        of the Remsen Street Diner
where Maria served up the best hot dogs
        and sauerkraut,
the gold cross hanging on her heavenly
        chest,
which I bent and touched, swearing
        I would never go back.

# WORKING THE COUNTER AT
# THE COHOES DRIVE-IN

Those nights at the drive-in, when
Johnny Michaels touched any breast
he wanted, when I heard Irene and Jeannette,
and Karen with the great ass, all talk
about Frank or Richie or Kevin, not one
of them saw me as I handed over popcorn,
jujube fruits and soft cups of RC. At intermission,
when they all slid from their half-opened
doors, tucking their shirts in, adjusting
their bras, their belts, I peered from the mosquito-
laden air of the dingiest yellow bulb in the world,
by the corner of the white-washed concrete bunker
where red neon signs flashed Hot Dogs, flashed Coca-Cola,
and I waited, pressed, starched white, starved
for one little feel.
                        As they stumbled
into the light like ghosts, I saw the screen rise
into the night, where candy-counter girls, dressed
in red and white stripes, walked off the edges
into the stars, and I saw the cars placed
like tanks ready to mount the small hills
upon which they were haphazardly parked,
a rear light flaring because someone's still-
passion-driven foot kicked the brake, a horn
blaring, a tossing body's mistake, knifing
its sudden shriek into the nerve-filled night
where abandoned headphones hung limply from poles,
their small voices speaking endlessly into the drive-in's dark.

IV

# STANDING IN THE NARROW NECK

Every December I come here and add
up the wrongs, the few things I've done
right, mumbling mea culpa, mea culpa,
and with the words comes the incense,
Father swaying around to hand me the gold
chalice and chain, the saints'
red and blue and yellow and white
light straining through the stained
glass windows, flooding my hands, my face,
so alive at times that I tried to shake
it off. Et cum spiritu tuo
and where's the spirit now
in this cold, I wonder, looking at the old
goldenrod stalks capped with snow,
the bare maples, oaks, the few
spruces genuflecting to a north wind. Nothing
moves until the host is raised again, held
before the crucifix, large white wafer
the size of this winter sun that floats
in the five p.m. Pennsylvania darkening
where, now, as though to some swinging
bell, white flakes start to drift
from the blank sky, making me say
Lord, it is time, and Lord, I am not
worthy, making me hum, loudly, sinner
that I am, as I walk home under
the first candles of evening.

# RUNNING THE TRAINS AT HIGH SPEED

The Reading whooshes by with its light
cutting across the boy's head, then the L & N,
the Southern Pacific, yellow cars, rust cars, coal
cars clickety-clacking while I push and pull
the switches for track changes and lights
to burst onto empty stations. Go faster, faster,
my son shouts and I open the throttle, shove
the red dial to High and sit back to watch
the trains take the curves at twenty miles
an hour, passing so quickly through Waterford,
Mechanicsville, through Troy and Amsterdam
I don't have time to point out the cliff
I dove seventy feet from into quarry water,
I can't say the name of the Cohoes Theater, the five
years of changing the marquee until that winter
of the great blackout when I was stuck up
on a ladder watching the streetlights pop
into February dark, leaving me there, high
and freezing, not wanting to die. Little
Richard blares from the Tavern House and
Tommy Edwards from Boney's, Butch DeSico
walks out into the back alley behind Jimmy's
and slams his fist through the garage door,
quietly bleeds to death in the snow falling.
My son's eyes are on green fire when the switch
light changes and all signs are Go, the wheels
sparking now with the lights out in the cellar,
only his face and my face hovering above the
rails where the whish and tick-tick-tick
of steel on steel sweep us further into
the city, down to the river where my brother

was raped, to Carlson's where three others
pulled knives, to Hathaway's Bakery where
my father embezzled money and my mother held
my hand in the manager's office, offered
me up as the one reason my father should not
be thrown into jail. Walking out past the cream
doughnuts, the double-layer cakes, I heard
even then, past the Mohawk and Hudson Rivers,
over the silver bridge where they met, that
thin whining screech of a whistle the black
train made as it rolled through the coins
my father had stolen, the coins I had stolen
back from his breadman's leather purse every night.
It comes round and round again, the engine's
lights exploding the dark, the Baltimore & Ohio,
the Santa Fe, the distant names my son cries out,
trying to touch the caboose that always goes by
too fast, the workmen inside nothing
but small blurs as they sit at their lantern-
lit table, not one of them waving, not one
of them looking out.

## WINDOW ON HVAR

Snow on the three tiers, the stone row
glistening through the December bare
trees, maple, oak, the red tufts of
poison sumac hanging on, the way we
hang on here in our bedroom, you still
in sleep, me staring at some invisible
face, twirling my hands in hair that
is not there, thinking twenty years,
thinking time pushing us forward,
always forward.
        In that other country,
that other year, you slept with your
ring hand touching your cheek, young,
innocent, and out that window I saw
a wineboat, men working into dawn, a
few of them already singing for the day
that lay ahead, one stripping off his shirt
in six a.m. and diving into the glistening
Adriatic. And beyond them more shining
on waves, the channel, the limestone
cliffs, and what, What? I asked aloud,
and you stirred, stretched and yawned,
opened your blue and green eyes, unseeing,
still in sleep, calling my last name before
you turned your warm body back to the wall.

# WHAT NEXT?

Now that I know where the glasses
are kept, the plates, the knives
and forks and spoons, and I know
most of the faces in the pictures
that stare from the various shelves,
some of their lives, who they supposedly
loved, what next? And now that you
have seen my coin trick, the giant
snow man I build every winter, heard
the hesitant cough of my heart
that is so much my father's, what more
do you expect?
            This is all the world
is, my friend said on the telephone last
night, and I said Yes, Yes,
tasting the chilled grapefruit and gin
on my tongue again, feeling the lace
of your red and black camisole, letting
my mind enter that space where our bodies
touched, feeling the sweat there, and
the love and the hate, the sudden flaring
up and the settling, always the settling,
        back into the dark.

# THE BLACK WINGS

All winter the light fluff of blue, gray, or brown
fur and feathers drifting on the morning porch
signaled the death of some bird or mouse, the small
feet and empty skins left for us as a gift from our
cats, surprisingly little blood. Just
yesterday the wind knocked and I opened the door
to a rabbit half-eaten, its shiny guts hanging out,
still alive, steaming, its glazed eyes unblinking,
the same absence I had seen in my grandfather's eyes
that night he stood in the living room trying
    to say goodbye,
telling me to check the oil before I began the long drive
back, the black wings growing from his shoulders, spreading
in that small room until I could not breathe and so
told him I had to leave, and he nodded, said he understood.
Standing on our winter porch, I looked around
to see if they were gathering here, about
the white house, I stared at the blue-gray iron clouds,
the arcing, dried branches of the forsythia hedge,
but did not sense them, not yet. And when
they come, I said aloud, wanting them to know
I knew who they were, it had better be for me, Me
I shouted, suddenly furious, my entire body tight, hard,
refusing to turn around although I could hear my wife
and son knock on the window, steadily tapping,
calling me in from the February cold.

# JOSHUA'S TENT

My son cries three, four times, wakes
me with the shrill edge of his voice
yelling Bear, and Wait, mumbling words
under his covers I cannot make out, and
I yell back into his room, It's all
right, although I know it isn't, for
he sees the large grizzly that will eat his heart,
the emerald-green snake that coils
with its tail in its mouth. When he doesn't
stop, I go into his night-light dark,
a shadow among shadows, and I bend
to unzip his bed-tent and enter,
head first, leaving behind the day
of cutting grass and painting shutters,
growing again into his warm breathing,
his skin glow in the caul of the tent
where his eyes finally close, at peace
    in dream
because his father's come to sleep with him.

# MIDWINTER

Going down to throw another
log into the stove, I saw the brass
glint of the barometer my good
friend gave us this past winter, and
I tapped it hard, in the uncertain
light, winced my eyes up and tried
to see if the directional arrow
had moved since the day before.
Nothing. Not one millimeter, and
I thought of his twenty-five years
of madness, and of his other
twenty-five years of chosen snow-
isolation, of his cracked mind
and his shaking hands and his
heavy white cups of coffee, his
white cigarette butts piled
in the glass ashtray. And
I stood there in the middle
of a hard winter trying to make
sense of it again, and again
failing, able only to stare out
at the frozen pond, finally hear
the tap-tapping of the ice-sheathed
maple branches that had been clattering
senselessly all the while.

# SHOVELING WHILE THE SNOW KEEPS FALLING

How many times have I found myself
out here shoveling while the flakes
keep falling, the low rumble of my voice
like that of the shovel as it scrapes
the pitted concrete, my wife's
words in my ears, Why go out
while it's still snowing? I can't
tell her my father comes back
when it snows like this, his brown collar up,
the flakes caught in his big wave of hair
where they slowly crumple and melt. That he walks
down close to the house, especially
at night, bowing through
the spruce, knocking clumps of snow
from branches in small, explosive
puffs. I used to think he wanted to talk
about his wife, my mother,
about the day she left and he stood
by the canal fence and wept, but instead
he whispers the shine of the
'52 Buick, tells me he lit candles
as an altar boy, then asks the names
of the presidents again, says the next
time he comes he'll expect me to know
the states and their capitals, the ones
I've been repeating the past thirty
years of my life. When he squats and makes
drawings in the snow I can't see clearly,
he tells me he knows I've been fucking
up, but it's all right, he can tell

I'm learning to open myself despite
the fearful dreams my mother still
breathes into my head of my wife leaving
with another man, of my sons and
daughters being hit by a speeding
car. It's not easy, he sighs,
waving his hands in the blue-black
air as though they were wind, telling
me as I straighten my back
that I cannot afford to stop and talk,
just keep shoveling no matter
how cold my toes get, no matter
how many times the snow covers
the clean walk.

# WHAT THE HELL

I split maple and oak, birch and shagbark
hickory, heave the ax up with murderous
intent, angry again at something, having to stop
before I can figure out what. I count them up,
the unpaid bills, the arrogant boss, not even enough
money to have a birthday party for my son. What
the hell, I shout, without knowing I'm doing
it, then shout it louder, What the hell,
pleased with hearing it echo off
the barn, down around the pond
and across the road into my neighbor's house.
It doesn't even sound like my voice,
I think, taking off my woolen hat
so I can hear it better, waving to my wife
who has come to the door, telling
her to go back in, I'm all right. And as soon
as she's gone, I shout it again, breathing
easier now, my back only half
an ache as the dogs start to bark and my son
stares out the window at his father
who kicks snow and throws chunks
of wood into the gray sky-cloud,
turns to face the north wind
that has thumped his back all morning.

# NOVEMBER, WASSERGASS

As soon as he's out the door
the cats scatter and the dog howls, tail
between legs, half-hobbling, half-running
into the shadow of the barn, my three-year-old
boy soon after him, maple branch whip raised
in the November air, the terror of Wassergass.
When he comes back, he has a sword
he's found in the garage sale pile,
the one with a cat's head in black surrounded by red,
and he's slashing at my legs as I rake yellow and green
    leaves into a pile for burning.
Down, he shouts, Down, and I fall, slowly,
in case there are sharp sticks in the leaves, and I close
my eyes, pretend I am dead. In the new silence
the leaves smell fresh, the moist smell of roots and dirt,
and my dead father rises from the damp ground again,
the dust of him making me cough the way he coughed,
the holes in his skin showing me the dark.
I can hear his breathing, like wind
over the leaves, my father's thin lips, still
wet from drinking gold beer, brushing
my ears with words I listen to as long
as I can: Stay down, rest, he says,
For every hour of joy, there's twenty-three of ruin,
Cain killed his brother, didn't he? Do you
remember the yellow piss stains on my bed,
the night I gave you two of my last four dollars,
Even my bones are dust now, even my bones
and I find myself nodding Yes, Yes to everything he says,
    the thin
rustle of my head shaking in the leaves finally
bringing me back, my eyes opening to see nothing
but leaves, brushing them off beneath branches
that tremble in what seems to be complete confusion,
where my son's face suddenly appears, looking down,
smiling at his father who is looking up.

# MY FATHER'S NAME

It's done. I've tied the wreath
        to the top
of the gravestone with the stiff
        blue wires, twisted
their ends together in the ten below
        zero, my fingers
burning dull red like the candles
        that flickered
at my father's funeral.
And I've prayed to the God I don't
        know
exists, asked Him to protect
        my living
son, unable to count on it,
my mind drifting into the cold pines
        at the end
of the field where my Aunt Eleanor
        dies seven years of Alzheimers,
where my father drinks his way
through five Buicks, Oldsmobiles and
        Chevrolets,
ends up walking down Ontario Street
holding his heart that finally bursts.
I have lifted my eyes to the Lord
        and seen cirrus clouds
in the upstate New York cold
blowing northwest to east, as they always
        did,
seen my mother for the thousandth-
        thousandth time,
her white hands clenched on the window
        sill, afraid

for years to leave the house,
seen myself standing with stone angels
    for another hour, unable
to even bend and straighten the wreath
    which the wind has crooked,
floundering on the third row, the seventeenth
    grave,
for a few cold seconds forgetting
    my father's name.

# THE RED PLASTIC KEY

My son walked from door to door, the
red plastic key held in his hand so
he could unlock each one and enter
to find his sister still asleep,
his father reading a book in bed, his
mother missing until he heard
the radio's hum downstairs in
the kitchen. I want to unlock
your heart, he said, climbing
onto my lap, and I nodded, not
caring that he screwed
the red key into my chest,
tried to shove it in, while
I thought of all the names and faces
that would come pouring out,
the green hate, the voices
rising through a ceiling that no longer
existed, the dream in which
my wife, my children were swept
downstream in a river's flood. When
I came back I could feel nothing,
although my son was still pushing,
putting all of his three-year-old
body into each jab, neither of us
surprized when the skin broke
and small beads of blood bubbled
up like rain drops on a window,
growing larger and larger until
they trickled down and pooled
on my stomach, small pond
of blood in which my son
and I dipped our fingers
and dabbed each other's faces
with smeared signs of love.

# THE FIRST WOMEN I TOUCHED

In the light of the window that faced the street
they were the first women I touched, one with ballet
slippers, the left foot arched, pointed to the floor,
her underpants rolled halfway down
her hips, the other sitting straight
in a chair, her lace-covered legs folded
as she pursed her dark lips, absorbed
in a thin book she held before her flower-wreathed breasts.
This was before my brother had gone to Okinawa,
when he hid these women in his sock drawer,
before he parachuted into the sun and lost
his mind, before he was electro-shocked thirty-seven
times in the first months of his madness
that has lasted the past twenty-three years
of his life. This was when my father's blue-gray
Oldsmobile stood shining by the canal fence,
when he walked out the door in a white shirt and wide paisley
        tie, holding my mother's white gloved hand.
This was before the morning I heard them talking at the kitchen
        table
to my brother who had just come back from the war,
their quiet whispering giving away the suffering
clearly as I stood on the cold hall stairs.
This was before I answered the door to a fat Irishman named Terry
who was crying in the rain, the black car heavily idling smoke
        behind him,
before he said he loved my mother, Was she home?
This was before the stories my life has become,
before my first kiss, before I even dreamed of entering
        a woman,
before I slept an entire night with a woman whispering my name,

before I heard a woman peeing in the toilet,
before a woman ever cooked me an egg.
This was before my second world began, the one from which I look
    back
and remember two women in a postcard picture, one of them
            wrapping
her white arms finally around me in a room where handkerchiefs
    were the smoothest silk,
where stockings were a fine black mesh
that swished her flesh as she drew them off.

# FOR THE DEAD SONS

Reading the man's poem
about his son, Sam, and
grapes, and the first jug
of water, and the empty boxes
    of shells,
I remember now his son is
dead, just a few years ago,
    young dead,
and I think of my Joshua
four hundred miles from here,
    wonder
if he is riding the yellow car
we bought him for Christmas,
if he is eating his tomato
soup and crackers as he sits
watching another cartoon on the
    VCR.
And I think of the other poet's
    son, flung
from a mountain at nineteen,
and another's, given back
    at seven,
and my friend's son hit
    by the speeding Buick,
his head breaking open on the
    road, and I
try to hear their final sounds,
    each one different,
a scream, a sigh, perhaps
calling to their fathers for help
because they have always been so strong,
and their fathers standing there,
all of the fathers standing there,
    helpless, as their sons die.

# THE TRUTH

My father walks in with the dirt smell
of the roads all over him, sits with
the gold glass of Schaefer's and pours
the coins from his leather purse, nickels,
dimes, pennies, quarters piled in a mound
that we separate and count and roll. But
tonight he is not whistling, he is not
rolling twenty quarters in two seconds
with two fingers, and he is telling me
his busted knuckle is from a softball,
not a punch, the holes in his face from
pimples, not jungle rot. He is slicing
his left hand although I cannot
believe it, lifting it onto the metal
table and telling me he bleeds like anyone else.
When I get up to put on the Tommy Edwards'
album, he coughs, says I love her,
I love her, although she's
in another town with her fat Irishman,
resting on the Mediterranean couch
without one thought of him. Listen,
he shouts, as I start to move in the circles
he taught me, I'm a bum, a drunk,
and he holds my chin up so I must look
into the bloodshot eyes, his greased-back
hair, the holes in his face dark as caves,
see the kitchen light that glares
behind him, his shadow up there on the tin
ceiling where vines tangle and untangle,
where thick white clusters of flowers bloom.

# THE NATIONAL POETRY SERIES 1988

*Black Wings*
Len Roberts
Selected by Sharon Olds/Persea Books

*After We Lost Our Way*
David Mura
Selected by Gerald Stern/E.P. Dutton

*Great Bird of Love*
Paul Zimmer
Selected by William Stafford/University of Illinois Press

*Green the Witch Hazel Wood*
Emily Hiestand
Selected by Jorie Graham/Graywolf Press

*Constant Mercy*
Lee Upton
Selected by James Tate/Atlantic Monthly Press

The National Poetry Series was established in 1978 to publish five collections of poetry annually through five participating publishers. The manuscripts are selected by five poets of national reputation. Publication is funded by the Copernicus Society of America, James A. Michener, Edward J. Piszek, The Lannan Foundation, and the five publishers—E.P. Dutton, Graywolf Press, Atlantic Monthly Press, Persea Books, and the University of Illinois Press.